TELL THE

TELL THE

Story

Foreword by Jimmy Scroggins

Edited by Mark Warnock and
Jean A. Albert

Scripture quotations are from the ESV® Bible (The Holy Bible, English Standard Version®), copyright © 2001 by Crossway, a publishing ministry of Good News Publishers. Used by permission. All rights reserved.

ISBN-13: 978-1539495864
ISBN-10: 1539495868

Published by CreateSpace for Family Church Media.

1101 S Flagler Drive
West Palm Beach, FL 33401
www.gofamilychurch.org

TABLE OF CONTENTS

v

FOREWORD

By Jimmy Scroggins, Lead Pastor, Family Church

Our church has a rich tradition of celebrating Christmas. For decades our congregation put on a musical extravaganza called "The Singing Christmas Tree." "The Tree," as our members affectionately called it, became an institution in our community – part of the way that our entire city celebrated Christmas. Hundreds of people were engaged in the production, and thousands of people came each year to hear the music, experience the drama, and listen to the message. From beginning to end, the message was clear – Christ has come! Through that event many people came to know Jesus and many people were introduced to our church.

I believe that the event resonated so strongly with so many because the music made people *feel something*. Artistic expression has the power to make us do that – make us *feel something* in our hearts, *feel something* in our souls, feel something that we can't quite explain, *feel something* that makes us want to connect.

Even though our church doesn't do "The Tree" anymore, we have more artists and more pastors engaged in our church than ever before. And these gifted men and women have a passion to make us *feel something* about the story of Jesus. Last year our worship team produced an amazing collection of Christmas music called "Tell The Story" (available on iTunes, Google Play, and Amazon) and our pastors and ministry leaders wrote the devotional book you hold in your hands.

We hope you will use these stories, reflections, and devotional readings personally and with your family as you ponder the message that permeates our ministry – Christ has come!

Our church has changed a lot in recent years. And our celebration of Christmas has evolved as well. But one thing hasn't changed at all – we are still all about Jesus. So no matter what your past looks like, no matter what your family looks like, and no matter where you are in your faith journey – we want you to *feel something* this Christmas. We want you to engage with the message that God is reaching out to you. We want you to believe that Jesus came as a baby at Christmastime, grew up into a man, was crucified on a cross, and was raised from the dead. Christ has come, and He has come to make a difference in your life. So read, ponder, listen, share, and enjoy. Most of all, believe! Christmas reminds us that Christ has come!

Love and blessings to you and yours.
Pastor Jimmy

INTRODUCTION

The devotionals in this book were written by the pastors and ministry leaders of Family Church. They are a diverse bunch: Some are young, some older; some have been Christians for many decades, others are much newer to the faith; a few have seminary PhDs, others have no formal theological training. The men and women who have written these devotionals come from a variety of racial and cultural backgrounds, minister to different age groups, and each has their own unique voice. I think you'll be stimulated by the range of perspectives.

We have three hopes for this book.

First, we hope that it will help you dive deep into the story of Christmas. Most of us are familiar with the basics of the Christmas story: Jesus, born in a manger, announcing angels, trembling shepherds and seeking wise men. When we take a closer, unhurried look at some of these passages, though, we can discover some profound details about the way God works and about the mission of Jesus. We've written on the classic Christmas passages in Matthew and Luke, but have also included some Old Testament readings that prophesy the coming of Jesus. We want you to see how Jesus' coming is the fulfillment of God's plan from the very beginning.

Second, we hope that this guide will help you establish, re-establish or strengthen a daily quiet time with God. For centuries, men and women who have thrived in their relationship with God have made it a habit to read His Word and pray every day. In our busy world, doing that consistently is quite a challenge—especially during the busyness of Christmas. Even pastors can find their personal time with God squeezed out amidst the holiday buzz. As our world gets more frenzied, however, it is all the more important that Christians seek the Lord in "the secret place" and find in Him the strength and comfort we need to live with a peace the world cannot give us. So take thirty days to go on this journey with us, and by the end, you may find that meeting with God every day has become a habit. We pray so.

Third, we hope that you will be spurred on to "Tell the Story." The arrival of Jesus to rescue us is the greatest news the world has ever heard. We owe it to our friends and neighbors—and to Jesus—not to be silent, but to share His story, especially in this season.

There are thirty devotional readings in this book, designed to cover the season of Advent, which starts four Sundays before Christmas day. Each is written by a different pastor or ministry leader from Family Church. Each one has a Scripture passage printed for you to read, and a short reflection on that passage, along with a suggested prayer.

We have designed five of the thirty devotionals to be able to be used as simple Family Devotions—one for each of the four Sundays of Advent, and one for Christmas Eve or Christmas Day. One way to share the story is by sharing with your family. You may even want to invite some neighbors to participate in Family devotions with you.

The family devotionals include an option to play songs from our companion Christmas album, "Tell the Story," which is available on iTunes, Amazon, and Google Play. The music is terrific, and we think you'll enjoy it.

We have also included two appendices: one on how to have a quiet time with God, and another one on how to lead a successful Family devotion time. We hope you find them helpful.

I need to express my great gratitude to the devotional writers, the awesome pastors and ministry leaders of Family Church, who I get to work with every week. Jean Albert's sharp editorial eye was a tremendous help, as was the guidance of George Estornell and the Kids ministry team as we developed the Family Devotionals.

Now, as much as any time I can remember, the world needs— and we need—the peace and presence of Jesus. "We have seen his star in the east, and have come to worship him."

Merry Christmas,
Mark Warnock, Editor

First Week of
Advent

BUSTED!

Aaron Filippone

Genesis 3:14-15
"Because you have done this, cursed are you above all livestock and above all beasts of the field; on your belly you shall go, and dust you shall eat all the days of your life. I will put enmity between you and the woman, and between your offspring and her offspring; he shall bruise your head, and you shall bruise his heel."

Going to school wasn't the highest priority on my list as a kid. Most days, I would have done anything to be able to stay home from school. One morning, I decided that this was my big chance to skip school. As I was walking down the street developing my plan, I could hear the loud screeching sound of the air brakes. My heart began to beat out of my chest. I looked ahead and a dust cloud from the dirt road enveloped the big yellow bus. It was at that moment that I had a decision to make. I could run toward the bus and get on, or I could slow down and intentionally miss the bus. It didn't take me long to dart to the left and hide behind the big wooden telephone pole by Mr. Mock's house.

After what seemed like hours, the bus closed its doors and proceeded down the road towards Kingsford Elementary School. I turned around and started walking home. Before I could start working up fake tears and a story about missing the bus, I was met by my mother who was standing on the front porch watching the entire saga unfold.

3

Have you ever been found in your sin? It's a terrible feeling. Imagine what Adam and Eve felt like when they were busted. Imagine the guilt, the fear, the anxiety. They probably thought that the human race would be completely obliterated that day. But God had a different plan. In this incredible statement, God promises to send a rescuer who will defeat the devil and roll back the curse of sin and death. Scholars often call this passage the *protoevangelium*, literally the first mention of the gospel. Thousands of years later, God came through on his promise by sending Jesus as the atoning sacrifice for our sins.

I haven't found my kids skipping the school bus—yet—but I have caught them sinning. No matter how big or small their sins are, no matter how disappointed or embarrassed I am at their actions, one thing remains true. They are my kids and I could never stop loving them. In the same way, we who are in Christ have a heavenly father who can never stop loving us.

....

Dear God, thank you for keeping your promise to send Jesus. Today I confess my great need for you. Please forgive me for choosing my plan over yours. Thank you for continuing to love me in spite of my sin. Amen.

....

My thoughts and prayers...

_____

_____

_____

_____

_____

_____

_____

_____

_____

_____

_____

_____

_____

_____

_____

_____

Family Devotion Guide

Based on "Busted!" by Aaron Filippone

(For practical suggestions on how to lead a Family Devotional time, see Appendix Two.)

• Read the following passage:

Going to school wasn't the highest priority on my list as a kid. Most days, I would have done anything to be able to stay home from school. One morning, I decided that this was my big chance to skip school. As I was walking down the street developing my plan, I could hear the loud screeching sound of the air brakes. My heart began to beat out of my chest. I looked ahead and a dust cloud from the dirt road enveloped the big yellow bus. It was at that moment that I had a decision to make. I could run toward the bus and get on, or I could slow down and intentionally miss the bus. It didn't take me long to dart to the left and hide behind the big wooden telephone pole by Mr. Mock's house.

After what seemed like hours, the bus closed its doors and proceeded down the road towards Kingsford Elementary School. I turned around and started walking home. Before I could start working up fake tears and a story about missing the bus, I was met by my mother who was standing on the front porch watching the entire saga unfold.

- Discuss: How do you feel when you get caught doing something wrong?

- Explain that Adam and Eve got caught sinning in the Garden of Eden. God had commanded them not to eat the fruit of the tree of knowledge of good and evil, but when the serpent tempted Eve, both Adam and Eve ate the fruit. This verse is what God said to the serpent.

- Read Genesis 3:14-15:

"Because you have done this, cursed are you above all livestock and above all beasts of the field; on your belly you shall go, and dust you shall eat all the days of your life. I will put enmity between you and the woman, and between your offspring and her offspring; he shall bruise your head, and you shall bruise his heel."

- Read the following passage:

Have you ever been found in your sin? It's a terrible feeling. Imagine what Adam and Eve felt like when they were busted. Imagine the guilt, the fear, the anxiety. They probably thought that the human race would be completely obliterated that day. But God had a different plan. In this incredible statement, God promises to send a rescuer—the woman's offspring—who will defeat the devil and roll back the curse of sin and death. Scholars often call this passage the protoevangelium, literally the first mention of the gospel.

Thousands of years later, God came through on his promise by sending Jesus as the atoning sacrifice for our sins.

- Discuss: Why did Jesus come?

- Listen to "O Come O Come Emmanuel" from Tell the Story Christmas album from Family Church Worship (optional).

- Have a family member read this prayer aloud:

Dear God, thank you for keeping your promise to send Jesus. Today we confess our great need for you. Please forgive us for choosing our plans over yours. Thank you for continuing to love us in spite of our sin. Amen.

CREATED WITH A PURPOSE

Tim Akin

Isaiah 49:5-6
And now the LORD says, he who formed me from the womb
to be his servant, to bring Jacob back to him; and that Israel
might be gathered to him—for I am honored in the eyes of the
LORD, and my God has become my strength— he says: "It is
too light a thing that you should be my servant to raise up the
tribes of Jacob and to bring back the preserved of Israel; I will
make you as a light for the nations, that my salvation may
reach to the end of the earth."

Have you ever felt you were made for a specific reason or with
a particular mission to accomplish in life? Perhaps you believe
that you were made to be a mom or dad, a husband or wife, an
athlete or artist, a teacher or a doctor, a pastor or a professor.
Eric Liddell, a Scottish 400-meter gold medalist in the 1924
Olympics and a missionary, believed that God made him for
a purpose. He said, "God made me fast and when I run I feel
his pleasure." Liddell used his God-given talent as an athlete
to accomplish the mission of preaching the Gospel of Jesus
Christ in his home country of Scotland and as a missionary
to China.

In Isaiah 49:5-6 we read a prophecy about "the Servant of the
Lord," who was born for a specific reason and to accomplish
a particular mission. In fact, He was confident that God
had prepared Him for His mission from the womb, and He
believed that this task would be accomplished.

9

This "Servant" is revealed to us in the New Testament as Jesus Christ, the "Lamb of God who takes away the sins of the world." Here, Isaiah is teaching us that Jesus was created for the purpose of redeeming all people from their sins and what a great mission this is.

In Acts 13:47, St. Paul paraphrases Isaiah 49:6 when he says, "I have made you a light to the Gentiles, that you may bring salvation to the ends of the earth." When a person repents of their sins and believes in Jesus Christ, they are made into a new creation, they are born again, and they are given a new purpose and a new mission in this life. All Christians are given the mission of being ambassadors for Christ, and calling people to be reconciled to God. Are you living out your life's mission?

....

Dear Jesus, thank you for saving me from my sins, and for being a light to all nations. Give me the strength to accomplish your mission of being your ambassador and sharing with those far from God how to be reconciled to Christ. Please use me as a missionary where I live, work, and play. Amen.

....

My thoughts and prayers...

PRINCE OF PEACE

Bill Keith

Isaiah 9:6
For to us a child is born, to us a son is given; and the
government shall be upon his shoulder, and his name
shall be called Wonderful Counselor, Mighty God,
Everlasting Father, Prince of Peace.

Christmas is the most wonderful time of the year! Parties, festivals, concerts, family reunions, gifts, and the greatest gift of all God's Son, Jesus, the Savior of the world. The Prince of Peace.

Everyone desires inner peace. The Bible describes the peace that God gives as "the peace that passes all understanding." People will do anything for peace in relationships, peace at work, and peace in their homes. They look for it in so many places, in so many things, yet they never find true peace. Only God can give lasting peace.

I'm reminded of a true story of four men and their wives returning home from a business conference in Atlanta. They were very late and were in a hurry to make their flight at the airport. As they were running to their gate, they rounded a corner and ran into a table full of crystal vases. The vases hit the floor and broke into pieces. They apologized as they continued their quick pace to make their flight. Finally at the gate, one of the men said, "I must go back and make what we did right. I'll catch the next flight and see you at home".

With that he turned and left in search of the spot where the vases had been shattered. There he found a lady on her knees, feeling for the vases and cutting her fingers on the broken pieces. As he knelt down and began to help her, he realized that she was completely blind. Helping her to a chair, he apologized for what had happened, and gave her $100 to cover the damage. She was weeping softly and she said, "Thank you. Are you Jesus?" He replied, "No, but I believe in Him."

This Christmas, take the time to stop in the midst of the busyness and demands to focus on the One we celebrate. Read the Bible and talk to God for "great peace have they whose mind is stayed on Him." Galatians 5:22-23 says the result of His presence in our lives is love, joy, peace, patience, kindness, goodness, faithfulness, gentleness, and self-control. Let's not forget to let the Prince of Peace shine through our lives.

....

Today, I come to you Lord Jesus. I pray that this Christmas will be the most peaceful I've ever known. As I draw close to you, understanding that you are the Prince of Peace, help me to be an example of that peace to others. In Jesus' name, Amen.

....

My thoughts and prayers...

_____

_____

_____

_____

_____

_____

_____

_____

_____

_____

_____

_____

_____

_____

_____

_____

LIVING BY FAITH

Charles Burgan

Luke 1:30-33
And the angel said to her, "Do not be afraid, Mary, for you have found favor with God. And behold, you will conceive in your womb and bear a son, and you shall call his name Jesus. He will be great and will be called the Son of the Most High. And the Lord God will give to him the throne of his father David, and he will reign over the house of Jacob forever, and of his kingdom there will be no end."

Mary's life was forever changed when God's angel spoke to her, delivering the news that she would give birth to the King of kings, our Lord and Savior Jesus Christ. This news raised many questions for Mary, but in the end, she declared that she was the Lord's servant and was willing to be obedient to God's plan. She knew that she did not need to carry fear like a weight around her neck, but knew instead to rely on her faith in God.

God often puts us in situations that feel overwhelming and all-consuming. But if we listen to what He is telling us and trust Him to guide our lives, we will find a peace that can only be found in the hands of our Lord and Savior. He has a plan for us. When we keep our eyes open, and our minds "stayed upon Him" we can find peace and conquer the fears that hold us back from the full blessing He has for us.

Perhaps the most important part of our walk with Christ is having complete faith in Him. Faith does not always come easy as it is not seen or felt, but when we are obedient, the blessings outweigh the questions and uncertainty. Faith helps us walk the narrow path He has set before us, and keeps us close in our walk with Him.

God wants to transform your life forever. Turn over all your fears and rest in faith that He already has a great and glorious plan for you, just like He did for Mary.

....

Dear God in heaven, I ask that you give me the strength to conquer my fears and that everyday my faith in you will grow stronger and stronger. God, you are in control and I pray that you will help me to have the faith of Mary. Amen.

....

My thoughts and prayers...

FAITHFUL

Johanna Jurado

Luke 1: 34-38
And Mary said to the angel, "How will this be, since I am a virgin?" And the angel answered her, "The Holy Spirit will come upon you, and the power of the Most High will overshadow you; therefore the child to be born will be called holy—the Son of God. And behold, your relative Elizabeth in her old age has also conceived a son, and this is the sixth month with her who was called barren. For nothing will be impossible with God." And Mary said, "Behold, I am the servant of the Lord; let it be to me according to your word." And the angel departed from her.

When an angel of the Lord told Mary she was going to give birth to God's one and only Son, she was confused. How could she have a baby? She was only a teenager and didn't even have a husband yet. Mary questioned the angel, just like many of us question God when we are facing an impossible situation.

But, even though Mary didn't fully understand the situation, she responded in a way that we can learn from. First, even though she had questions, doubts, and fears, Mary trusted and obeyed in what God had promised. Second, she was willing to obey rapidly and humbly no matter how difficult the situation. It is hard to accept situations that seem impossible, but we know we can rely on our faith in Jesus no matter what is in front of us.

Mary's faith allowed her to accept that she was going to give birth to Jesus. She held on to her faith even when people around her didn't understand what she was going through. She held on to her faith even when she felt unsure and it was hard to carry on. Often, instead of facing tough situations, we tend to avoid them. What if Mary had avoided her difficult and confusing situation? We would have missed out on something amazing --Jesus!

Many of us face difficult circumstances throughout our lives, but don't have the fearlessness or willingness to readily accept the situation. By avoiding hard situations, we might miss out on something marvelous that God has in store. Sometimes God brings us through tough times so we can love and trust Him more. After all, He's God and He has our best interests in mind. We should be like Mary: willing and ready to humbly trust and obey.

....

Father, thank you for being the God of the impossible. There is nothing that you cannot do. Thank you for preparing our hearts and minds to accept the situations that have been brought our way. Thank you for never leaving or forsaking us. We ask for a greater capacity to trust you no matter how difficult things may be. May we be filled with faith instead of doubt through it all. Amen.

....

My thoughts and prayers...

_____

_____

_____

_____

_____

_____

_____

_____

_____

_____

_____

_____

_____

_____

_____

_____

OUR LOW ESTATE

Krystal Gutierrez

Luke 1:46-49
And Mary said, "My soul magnifies the Lord, and my spirit rejoices in God my Savior, for he has looked on the humble estate of his servant. For behold, from now on all generations will call me blessed; for he who is mighty has done great things for me, and holy is his name.

During the Christmas season, my thoughts always drift back to the miracle of Christ coming to dwell among us. The wonder of it all makes my imagination soar! Try to imagine this moment: Mary receives news from an angel that she will conceive and give birth to the Messiah. The Savior she had believed in would soon arrive. I'm sure that in her teenage mind it never occurred to her that the God of the universe would look down and choose her to be the vessel that He would use for His ultimate plan. I try to think about what her thought process would have been. "Oh. My. Soul. Is this really happening? #crazy." As a young teenager, she recognizes her low estate. Mary knew that she was a nobody and yet at the same time she trusted in the sovereignty of her Heavenly Father. Her response at such a young and fragile age is unbelievable. I can picture Mary's posture bowed in adoration with arms stretched out as she worships the Lord for what He has done. I can hear her sweet song rise as she sings to the Lord. I would have loved to be a fly on the wall at this very moment!

Personally, it is hard for me to think about this moment without remembering my personal faith. I am constantly humbled by the fact that God looked down on my low estate and said, "Mine!" His great love for mankind is evident through the miracle of sending His only Son to dwell among us. Praise God for all that He has done!

....

Dear Lord, thank you for Jesus! Help me to be mindful during this Christmas season of the incredible miracle of Jesus coming down to meet me in my low estate. May my response always be to worship and adore you for all the things you have done and will do in my life. Teach me to trust in your sovereignty. Amen.

....

My thoughts and prayers...

_____

_____

_____

_____

_____

_____

_____

_____

_____

_____

_____

_____

_____

_____

_____

_____

REDISCOVER THE FAMILIAR

Derek Simpson

Matthew 1:18-20
Now the birth of Jesus Christ took place in this way. When his mother Mary had been betrothed to Joseph, before they came together she was found to be with child from the Holy Spirit. And her husband Joseph, being a just man and unwilling to put her to shame, resolved to divorce her quietly. But as he considered these things, behold, an angel of the Lord appeared to him in a dream, saying, "Joseph, son of David, do not fear to take Mary as your wife, for that which is conceived in her is from the Holy Spirit."

Living in South Florida, it's easy to become accustomed the beauty of the sun setting over perfectly framed palm trees or the brilliant blue water seascapes that surround us. However, sometimes the more familiar things become to us, the less amazing they seem. Every now and then, it's helpful for us pause and rediscover the familiar.

In Matthew 1:18-20 we read the incredible account of the birth of Jesus. If you've grown up in a Christian environment, or even if you haven't, you've likely read or heard this story dozens of times. It's easy to miss the miracle and majesty of this story if we become too familiar with it. Take a moment and read it again...slowly. What emotions must Mary have felt? Can you imagine being visited by an angel? What did Joseph think? Imagine the kind of faith he had to have!

As we go about the Christmas season, with all of its routines and tradition, let's take a fresh look at the story of Jesus' birth. Let's marvel at the miraculous way Jesus entered the world and ultimately, let it remind us of the miraculous way that Jesus re-entered the world after his crucifixion; from a baby in a manger to a resurrected King.

....

Father in Heaven, during this season of traditions and holiday routine, help us not to overlook the faith and obedience of Mary and Joseph. Thank you for the miraculous way that you sent the Savior of the world to earth and for the hope that we have because of His resurrection. Give us opportunities to help others find rescue and redemption in King Jesus. Amen.

....

My thoughts and prayers...

Second Week of
Advent

WAITING FOR HIS TIMING

Heather Khadij

Luke 2:1-6
In those days a decree went out from Caesar Augustus that all the world should be registered. This was the first registration when Quirinius was governor of Syria. And all went to be registered, each to his own town. And Joseph also went up from Galilee, from the town of Nazareth, to Judea, to the city of David, which is called Bethlehem, because he was of the house and lineage of David, to be registered with Mary, his betrothed, who was with child. And while they were there, the time came for her to give birth.

Have you marked up your calendar with your agenda? Have you listed off your daily tasks, errands, dreams, bucket lists, and priorities? We live in a world where we are all about making things happen in our timing. If you have an iPhone, have you ever asked Siri a question, waited five seconds for a response, and thought it took too long? I know that is true for me at times.

As I read this verse, I thought a lot about how Mary must have felt as the time suddenly came for her to give birth. Was she nervous or scared? Soon after being given the privilege to write about this verse, I learned that my husband and I are expecting our first child. That news shed a whole new light on this verse for me.

God is reminding us that His ways are higher than our ways, His thoughts are higher than our thoughts, and His timing is perfect, even when His timing does not match up with ours. Despite what Mary might have wanted, that 'time' was the perfect time for Jesus to be born.

The best part in all of this is that God is for us and not against us. God's timing is always perfect because it is the best possible thing for us. We may not see it, believe it, or accept it, but God is showing us that we live according to His plans and His timing, and He will be with us through it all.

God has our best interests in mind. He loves us more than we can think or imagine, and at just the right time, He will reveal His will for us.

....

God, thank you for loving me unconditionally. Thank you that you sent your Son, Jesus, to die on the cross for my sins, and that you raised Him to life three days later. I pray that I will continue to wait upon you and your timing, knowing everything will happen according to your will. Amen.

....

My thoughts and prayers...

_____

_____

_____

_____

_____

_____

_____

_____

_____

_____

_____

_____

_____

_____

_____

_____

Family Devotion Guide

Based on "Waiting for His Timing" by Heather Khadij

- Discuss: What are some things you don't like waiting for?

- Discuss: What is good about having to wait? (For example, if you are waiting for dinner, it's good to wait so that it's fully cooked when you eat it....)

- Discuss: How do you feel when you don't have to wait anymore?

- Read Luke 2:1-6:

In those days a decree went out from Caesar Augustus that all the world should be registered. This was the first registration when Quirinius was governor of Syria. And all went to be registered, each to his own town. And Joseph also went up from Galilee, from the town of Nazareth, to Judea, to the city of David, which is called Bethlehem, because he was of the house and lineage of David, to be registered with Mary, his betrothed, who was with child. And while they were there, the time came for her to give birth.

• Read the following passage:

As I read this verse, I thought a lot about how Mary must have felt as the time suddenly came for her to give birth. Was she nervous or scared? Soon after being given the privilege to write about this verse, I learned that my husband and I are expecting our first child. That news shed a whole new light on this verse for me.

God is reminding us that His ways are higher than our ways, His thoughts are higher than our thoughts, and His timing is perfect, even when His timing does not match up with ours. Despite what Mary might have wanted, that 'time' was the perfect time for Jesus to be born.

The best part in all of this is that God is for us and not against us. God's timing is always perfect because it is the best possible thing for us. We may not see it, believe it, or accept it, but God is showing us that we live according to His plans and His timing, and He will be with us through it all.

God has our best interests in mind. He loves us more than we can think or imagine, and at just the right time, He will reveal His will for us.

- Have a family member read this prayer aloud:

God, thank you for loving us unconditionally. Thank you that you sent your Son, Jesus, to die on the cross for our sins, and that you raised Him to life three days later. Help us to wait upon you and your timing, knowing everything will happen according to your will. Amen.

- Play "Go Tell It" from Tell the Story Christmas album from Family Church Worship (optional).

HIS NAME IS JESUS

Ray Underwood

Matthew 1:21
She will bear a son, and you shall call his name Jesus, for he will save his people from their sins.

Do you remember when the Angel of the Lord appeared to Joseph in a dream and told him that his fiancée, Mary, was going to have a baby? The Angel said, "She will bear a son, and you shall call his name Jesus, for he will save his people from their sins."

The name "Jesus" (or "Yeshua") means "Yahweh is salvation"; so in calling the baby "Jesus" they were saying that God was saving His people through Him. But the angel specifically said that He would save His people "from their sins." What does this mean, "He will save His people from their sins"? The Bible says that all of us have sinned (Romans 3:23). We have done things that were wrong, said things that were wrong, thought things that were wrong, and had attitudes that were wrong. Sin has numerous destructive effects in our lives. Sin makes us guilty before God for the wrongs we have committed. Sin enslaves us, and sin would separate us from God forever. But, when Jesus came "to save His people from their sins," these things were reversed!

God solved our sin dilemma by sending God the Son to become a man, Jesus Christ, who died on the cross as the sacrifice which paid for our sins.

1 Peter 2:24 says, "He Himself bore our sins in His body on the cross" so that we could be reconciled to God. Our God loved us and paid the penalty for our sins.

Jesus came as a baby, but he came as the Savior. God has continued throughout the ages to pursue a personal relationship with each one of us. He constantly takes the initiative and is constantly moving towards us. The message of Christmas is that God is pursuing you!

....

Father, thank you for the gift of your Son. Jesus, you are our Savior, our Redeemer and our Deliverer. Thank you that you paid the penalty for our sins and that you constantly pursue us for our good and for your glory. May the Christmas season always be in our hearts so that we can remember that you came to seek and save. In your name we pray, Amen.

....

My thoughts and prayers...

_____

_____

_____

_____

_____

_____

_____

_____

_____

_____

_____

_____

_____

_____

_____

_____

_____

A DECISION TO OBEY

David Ramos

Matthew 1:24-25
When Joseph woke from sleep, he did as the angel of the Lord commanded him: he took his wife, but knew her not until she had given birth to a son. And he called his name Jesus.

Joseph was obedient to God by following what the angel had told him to do even though it was going to be uncomfortable, would not look right to the people, or feel appropriate. Joseph did not consider his own feelings, thoughts, or emotions. He did not sit around thinking whether or not to obey. He was determined to obey God's commandments no matter the cost. His obedience had such a profound effect in history that even today we are reading his story, rejoicing about it, and reaping the benefits of it.

Just like Joseph, we should do as the Lord commanded us. In Matthew 28:19, Jesus said, "Go therefore and make disciples of all nations, baptizing them in the name of the Father and of the Son and of the Holy Spirit."

The holiday season is a great time to share memories, stories, and great times with neighbors, co-workers, family, and friends. It is a time when people open their hearts to be more generous, more passionate, and to grow closer to those they love. I can't think of a better time to share the gospel of Jesus Christ.

The question today is this: if you knew that your obedience to God was going to have eternal repercussions, with whom would you share the story of Jesus? How quickly would you obey Him? Would you care what they thought of you? Our obedience to God's commandments can make an eternal difference in other people's lives. Don't pay attention to how you feel about being obedient or how someone else may look at it. Just follow Him and trust that He will be with you.

....

Lord Jesus, help me today to be bold about your message, and to share your story with someone this holiday season. Help me be obedient to your word. Forgive me for the many times that I have not been obedient and help me follow you today more than yesterday. In the name of Jesus I pray, Amen.

....

My thoughts and prayers...

_____

_____

_____

_____

_____

_____

_____

_____

_____

_____

_____

_____

_____

_____

_____

_____

_____

_____

_____

_____

_____

A HUMBLE ENTRANCE

Steve Scalici

Luke 2:7
And she gave birth to her firstborn son and wrapped him in swaddling cloths and laid him in a manger, because there was no place for them in the inn.

Have you ever wondered why the Savior and King was born in a place where animals were kept? Or why He was then laid in the animals' food trough? "There was no room for them in the inn." Certainly, God could have orchestrated a more suitable birthplace and bed for Jesus. Surely, the King of kings deserved a birthplace more becoming of a king. He deserved the most elegant of surroundings. Kings of much less stature throughout history have enjoyed the comforts that came with the office. But maybe that's the point.

Everything about this verse illustrates humility. God's own Son made His appearance on earth in the humblest of settings. His unpretentious beginning communicates an amazing message to creation: the transcendent God lowered himself to come to us. Instead of coming to earth as a coddled, privileged ruler, Jesus was born in humility, as one of us. His humility makes him accessible. This humble act should increase our desire to serve Him and dedicate our lives to Him. I have close friends who aren't as accessible as the King of kings. If I go to their house, I get stopped by a security guard at the gate and have to be "approved" in order to come in.

Jesus' act of humility, which started with him coming down from the highest place of all to the lowest place and culminated with his death and ultimate resurrection, makes it so I am already "approved". I don't even have to show my ID. My name is already in His book.

....

Jesus, thank you for your example of humility. I know that you resist the proud and give grace to the humble. When I lack humility, help me to focus on the scene of your birth. I humble myself because you first humbled yourself. You came from the highest place in Heaven to be born as a baby. Then, you served man and died for me. No one is more humble than you. Help me to show humility in my daily life. Amen.

....

My thoughts and prayers...

_____

_____

_____

_____

_____

_____

_____

_____

_____

_____

_____

_____

_____

_____

_____

_____

FEAR NOT

Jamie Thomas

Luke 2:8-10
And in the same region there were shepherds out in the field, keeping watch over their flock by night, and the angel of the Lord shone around them, and they were filled with great fear. And the angel said to them "Fear not ..."

How many times in our lives have we been faced with something unknown or unexpected and feared it? I can say that in many cases, I have greatly feared new territory and unexpected situations like my unexpected change of vocation, my recent unexpected search for a new home for my family, and even the unexpected blessing of a third child! I am sure that seeing an angel appear at night was frightening and unexpected—definitely unknown territory for the shepherds. They were frightened until the angel told them, "Fear not," and they learned that the angels were there to share the news about Jesus. Consequently, they faithfully and obediently followed their instructions to find Him.

We, too, are only human and will fear the unexpected things in life. Many will fear a call in a new direction—into "unknown territory." But we are also given the good news of Jesus: He was sent as a baby in a lowly manger, was crucified on the cross for our sins, raised from the dead, and will return for His believers. What are we to fear if he has already conquered all sin?

If we can do as the shepherds did and have faith and believe, then when we are obedient and faithful to the Word and keep our eyes set on finding Him in all we do, we need not be afraid.

When life presents us with the "unknown" or the "unexpected," as it will, the Bible reminds us that much like the shepherds who were watching over their sheep, so is God watching over His sheep. We are His sheep and the Lord is our shepherd. We can trust Him and keep our hearts and minds on Him when experiencing fear because he has already overcome the world.

....

Dear God, when I am fearful, please help me to keep my eyes and heart on Jesus. Help me remember that He has conquered all things through the Gospel. Lord, you are my shepherd and you watch over me in all things. Help me to obey and not be afraid. Amen.

....

My thoughts and prayers...

GOOD NEWS

Don Chinquina

Luke 2:10b-11
For behold, I bring you good news of great joy that will be for all the people. For unto you is born this day in the city of David a Savior, who is Christ the Lord.

One wonders what the shepherds were thinking before the angel showed up. Perhaps they were sitting on the hill wondering how they ended up in a dead end job working the night shift. Were they bitter at their lot in life? Or did they accept their fate of being social outcasts? Perhaps they were reflecting on the choices they made that put them in this job. Perhaps they felt so unworthy that they were just grateful to have any job.

To be a shepherd was to be a social outcast. Yet, it was to these "misfits" that the angel came to deliver the Good News. Why did the angel appear to them on that hillside instead of in the temple where all the religious people were?

It is easy to answer that question today by pointing to the symbolism of the Great Shepherd gathering his lost sheep. However, I doubt that the shepherds saw it that way. They no doubt realized that they were the most unlikely recipients to receive such a glorious message. And yet, there the angel was, meeting them where they were, and delivering to them the Good News of Jesus' birth.

How many of us can relate to the shepherds? How many of us have felt the weight of our own sin during moments of quiet desperation? How many of us have felt unworthy as we lived a life with no purpose while trudging towards the inevitable end?

But then we saw it all change when we accepted Jesus! In one moment, our world filled with light when we realized the Good News: that God sent his Son to live and die for unworthy sinners so that all who believe in Him may have everlasting life!

....

Dear Father, thank you for sending your Son to die on the cross for my sins. I know how unworthy I am to receive such a gift. However, I am grateful for your patience and loving kindness. Thank you for meeting me where I was, and for showing me grace and mercy. I offer this prayer in the name of your son Jesus Christ. Amen.

....

My thoughts and prayers...

_____

_____

_____

_____

_____

_____

_____

_____

_____

_____

_____

_____

_____

_____

_____

_____

THE MOST BEAUTIFUL SCENE

Stana Cyran

Luke 2:12
"And this will be a sign for you: you will find a baby wrapped in swaddling cloths and lying in a manger."

The all-powerful God of the universe who could use anyone and do anything chose this unlikely scene for the coming of the Messiah. He sent an angel to shepherds who were working through the night with a message of the birth of our Savior. God chose a smelly manger—of all places—to be the birthplace of the King of kings. Why the shepherds? Why the manger? Why a helpless babe in swaddling cloths? Paintings, music, and plays all depict the nativity scene so beautifully... but this scene just doesn't seem right. In fact, it seems flat out unimpressive.

Though I doubt the shepherds thought it was unimpressive...

Can you imagine being chosen to hear such great news straight from an angel? Can you imagine being chosen to ease Mary and Joseph's doubts about their own angel encounters and confirm that their son was the Son of God? Can you imagine their hearts skipping a beat when they saw the sign the angels told them about: the baby wrapped in swaddling cloths and lying in a manger?

I bet those shepherds, stealing away in the night and leaving their sheep, were elated and in awe.

The Messiah had come! He is here with us and all things will be set right. God is with us!

The beauty in this scene isn't the baby, the manger, Mary, Joseph, or even the angels. God is what is beautiful in this scene. Our God kept His promise. He sent a Messiah, the Savior of the world, and it was every bit as beautiful and awe inspiring as any play, painting, or piece of music man could ever create to communicate what was taking place in that moment.

....

Dear God, thank you for taking the mundane scene of a baby being born with no one but shepherds to welcome Him into the most beautiful scene imaginable. Thank you for sending your Son Jesus to us and for making a way for your people. Thank you for being faithful to keep your promises and for reminding me that YOU make this ordinary scene something beautiful! In the name of Jesus, Amen.

....

My thoughts and prayers...

Third Week of
Advent

THE ANNOUNCEMENT

Kevin Saxton

Luke 2:13-14
And suddenly there was with the angel a multitude of the heavenly host praising God and saying, "Glory to God in the highest and on earth peace among those with whom He is pleased! "

Anyone who has ever spent time around a new parent knows that they are generally very excited. The topic of conversation at any given moment is almost certain to be about that new baby and how it has changed their life for the better. Now, imagine that new parent somehow knows their child will be the one to end poverty, or racism, or cancer; you can imagine that the excitement level would be so much higher.

When the Creator of the Universe sent His Son, Jesus, into the world, He knew that it was a greater event than any of us could ever imagine. That's why He announced it through an angel—a Warrior of Light—and then followed it up with a choir of heavenly hosts that had to be measured in multitudes.

But what about the audience for His announcement? Were they worthy of such a glorious show? Why did God choose to announce His Son's birth to a lowly, pitiful band of shepherds? Much like the way we announce our children's births to the ones who care the most, Jesus' birth was announced to the group that needed that message more than any other—those who knew their need for something greater than themselves.

This royal announcement could not fall on deaf ears because it was the message of the greatest hope that the world would ever know. Finally, after hundreds of years of waiting, there was now a very certain way to find peace with God! The weight of such an announcement ought to draw us to the same place as that heavenly host—we ought to praise God. And, our response must be that of the shepherds: awe and wonder that God would choose to reveal Himself to us.

....

Father God, may we find our joy in what brings you joy, and may our hearts be filled with overwhelming gladness as we think about the fact that your Son was sent into the world that we may find peace with you. May we realize the magnitude of the gift of Jesus and live our lives as a glad response to Him. In Jesus' name, Amen.

....

My thoughts and prayers...

_____

_____

_____

_____

_____

_____

_____

_____

_____

_____

_____

_____

_____

_____

_____

_____

Family Devotion Guide

Based on "The Announcement" by Kevin Saxton

- To set up the scripture passage, explain that when Jesus was born, God the Father was so excited he sent an angel choir to share the news.

- Read Luke 2:13-14:

And suddenly there was with the angel a multitude of the heavenly host praising God and saying, "Glory to God in the highest and on earth peace among those with who He is pleased!

- Parents: Tell the story of how you felt when your child/children were born.

- Discuss: How do you feel when you get good news?

- Read the following passage:

When the Creator of the Universe sent His Son, Jesus, into the world, He knew that it was a greater event than any of us could ever imagine. That's why He announced it through an angel—a Warrior of Light—and then followed it up with a choir of heavenly hosts that had to be measured in multitudes. But what about the audience for His announcement? Were they worthy of such a glorious show?

Why did God choose to announce His Son's birth to a lowly, pitiful band of shepherds? Much like the way we announce our children's births to the ones who care the most, Jesus' birth was announced to the group that needed that message more than any other—those who knew their need for something greater than themselves. This royal announcement could not fall on deaf ears because it was the message of the greatest hope that the world would ever know. Finally, after hundreds of years of waiting, there was now a very certain way to find peace with God! The weight of such an announcement ought to draw us to the same place as that heavenly host—we ought to praise God. And, our response must be that of the shepherds: awe and wonder that God would choose to reveal Himself to us.

- Play "Angels We Have Heard on High" from Tell the Story Christmas album from Family Church Worship (optional).

- Have a family member pray (or read the prayer below):

Father God, may we find our joy in what brings you joy, and may our hearts be filled with overwhelming gladness as we think about the fact that your Son was sent into the world that we may find peace with you. May we realize the magnitude of the gift of Jesus and live our lives as a glad response to Him. In Jesus' name, Amen.

RUN TO THE SAVIOR

Daniel Martin

Luke 2:15-16
When the angels went away from them into heaven, the
shepherds said to one another, "Let us go over to Bethlehem
and see this thing that has happened, which the Lord has made
known to us." And they went with haste and found Mary and
Joseph, and the baby lying in a manger.

It's amazing how busy this time of year can become with all of
our travel plans, secret shopping trips to surprise that "special
someone", extended family arriving from out of town, and the
kids being out of school. In a world that many of us already
find busy enough, we manage to push ourselves even harder,
exhausting every ounce of our strength in order to accomplish
each task along the way.

Our culture has families running in multiple directions during
the Christmas season, spending ourselves and our money in
hopes of pleasing others. At Christmas, I often find myself
neglecting Jesus rather than running towards Him with haste
as the shepherds did. There is something about Christmas
that beckons people to come to His manger. Before He ever
spoke the words, "Come to me all who are burdened and
heavy laden, and I will give you rest," His very presence as
an infant was drawing people from all walks of life simply to
come to Him.

Let's set aside our tasks and burdens, be astonished by what took place that blessed Christmas morning, and with great haste run to Jesus! We celebrate Christmas not because of Hallmark or vacation time, but because God wants all the people of the world to run to His Son Jesus.

....

Dear Lord Jesus, thank you for stepping down from heaven to be born in a manger. I thank you for the amazing grace you give and the sacrifice you made on the cross. In the commotion of this season, I ask that your Holy Spirit would guide me to seek your presence, the healing that you offer, and the rest that I can only find in you. Help me to run toward you. Amen.

....

My thoughts and prayers...

THE POWER OF CHRISTMAS MEMORIES

Jimmy Scroggins

Luke 2:19
But Mary treasured up all these things, pondering them in her heart.

Some of the best memories I have are connected with Christmastime. When I was a kid we always got together with grandparents and cousins and aunts and uncles, exchanged presents, ate amazing meals, sang Christmas carols, and shared family stories. My brothers and I groaned each year when my Dad made us read the Christmas Story from Luke 2 before we were allowed to open any gifts.

As I got older and eventually had a family of my own, it has been a joy to develop our own Christmas traditions. At our house we work through an Advent Calendar with our kids every December. We have special musical events and meaningful Christmas Eve celebrations with our church family. Those special traditions and times together make Christmas a special and powerful part of our family dynamic.

This year Kristin and I launched our first child out of the house. Our oldest boy, James, left to be a cadet at West Point. So this December, for the first time, many of our family traditions will seem like they are missing something because they will be missing him.

Even though we know James is where he is supposed to be, it is honestly a little sad for us. And since we have eight kids, we are aware that James is just the first to go. Over the next several years each Christmas season will see our home (and our van) become a little bit less crowded.

Of course, the Scroggins family isn't the only one that misses people during Christmastime. I would venture to say that almost every family in our church dabs a few tears away as we think about people we love and Christmases past. Those memories and those pictures on the wall help give us joy and keep us tethered to loved ones and times that are no more.

It is interesting to me that God anticipated the strong connection between Christmastime and special memories. In the aftermath of the very first Christmas, the Bible says, "But Mary treasured up all these things, pondering them in her heart." (Luke 2:19) When the angels and shepherds were gone, and Mary was left alone with her baby and her husband, she made up her mind to always remember the special things she had experienced. Not too many years later she had to launch her son, too. What kept her going when she missed him? What helped her hold on to her faith when he was killed? How did Mary make it? I can't help but think that this verse in the Bible is there to instruct us. Mary treasured up the special times in her heart.

There are times in all of our lives when we feel the presence of God more powerfully than others. There are times when God just seems more real. There are moments and seasons when He seems close.

We need to treasure these times and ponder them in our hearts because time moves on, people move on, and life moves on. These memories that God gives us can help us keep the faith. Faith that Jesus really is "God With Us" - the One who came to save us from our sins.

....

God, thank you that you have chosen to be our God and make us your people. Thank you that you have made us "family" in Jesus. Thank you for special moments and memories that help us to hold onto our faith, even when the changing seasons of life make us a little sad. Help us to treasure these things in our hearts. Thank you most of all for sending your Son Jesus at Christmastime - the one who was born, crucified, buried, and raised from the dead. We look forward to the day when He comes again. Amen.

....

My thoughts and prayers...

THEY HEARD, THEY SAW, THEY TOLD

George Estornell

Luke 2:20
And the shepherds returned, glorifying and praising God for all they had heard and seen, as it had been told them.

They Heard
The shepherds heard the "good news of great joy that will be for all the people" (Luke 2:10). These were ordinary men—even outcasts of that society—and God chose them to hear this news first. The angel told them the One who would come to rescue and save His people from sin was born. The Rescuer and Savior is Jesus, the Son of the living God.

They Saw
They responded in rapid obedience by going to find the child. They found Mary, Joseph, and the baby and told all those gathered there what the angels had said to them—that this child was the Savior of the world. Many people wondered what they were saying, but Mary treasured this truth in her heart.

They Told
Their response to encountering the Savior was to worship Him and to tell others of Him. The result of their obedience was that God filled them with great joy. The shepherds left glorifying and praising God for all they had heard and seen. I can relate to the shepherds. I was an unlikely messenger who was far from God, living my own life, and going my own way.

Yet when I heard the good news that Jesus died for my sins, was buried and God raised Him from the dead, I repented and believed in Him. I have seen Jesus radically change my life. It is now my joy to go and tell others about my Savior—the Savior of the world.

What about you? If you've heard and seen, will you go and tell?

....

God, thank you for sending your son Jesus to rescue and save me from my sins. I pray that you would help me to be obedient as the shepherds were by going and telling others of the good news of great joy for all people. Amen.

....

My thoughts and prayers...

_____

_____

_____

_____

_____

_____

_____

_____

_____

_____

_____

_____

_____

_____

_____

_____

WAITING ON THE LORD

Bev Bonner

Luke 2:34-35
And Simeon blessed them and said to Mary his mother,
"Behold, this child is appointed for the fall and rising of many
in Israel, and for a sign that is opposed (and a sword will pierce
through your own soul also), so that thoughts from many hearts
may be revealed."

Five hundred years before Jesus was born, the prophet
Jeremiah wrote, "The Lord is good to those who wait for him,
to the soul who seeks him. It is good that one should wait
quietly for the salvation of the Lord."

Israel had been promised a Messiah and throughout Hebrew
history we see great men and women of faith who trusted in
that promise. Abraham, Moses, Joshua, Rahab, Joseph, Esther,
and many others had one thing in common; they believed the
promises of God and lived out their days in pursuit of Him.
They were a people with a rich legacy of faith that could be
traced back thousands of years and yet, when the time came
for the promise to be fulfilled, there were but a few who were
looking with expectancy.

Simeon had been waiting for the fulfillment of the prophecy
that the Messiah would come and the personal message he
had received from the Holy Spirit that he would not see death
until he had seen the Lord's Christ.

His account is part of the Christmas story as he lifts up the child Jesus and offers Mary and Joseph a prophetic blessing about their son and salvation for all people. Even so, the prophecy offered to them proclaims the great divide that Jesus would bring, as some would believe and others would not.

Just as Simeon received the fulfillment of what was promised to him, Jesus will fulfill his promise to us as we hope in Him. We are living out our days with the earnest expectation that as we have put our faith in the death, burial, and resurrection of Jesus Christ, we not only experience salvation and peace in this life, but also in the eternal life to come. On that day, when everything is fulfilled, Jesus will return as the great warrior King and make all things right!

....

Lord Jesus, may we have full assurance of our faith and look on with great anticipation and expectancy for that day when we will see you face to face and live in perfect peace. Amen.

....

My thoughts and prayers...

THE IMPORTANCE OF JESUS

Winner Olmann

Matthew 2:1-2
Now after Jesus was born in Bethlehem of Judea in the days of Herod the king, behold, wise men from the east came to Jerusalem, saying, "Where is he who has been born king of the Jews? For we saw his star when it rose and have come to worship him."

It may strike us as odd that wise men would travel from the east to Jerusalem just to see a baby. Could it be that there was something so significant about this newborn that wise men would consider it nothing to go out of their way and journey such a great distance? This brief passage clearly shows us that this child, born in Bethlehem, was no ordinary child.

The wise men from the east recognized who Jesus was. They understood that Jesus, although an infant, was born a king. And not only was he born a king, but he was born "king of the Jews", God's chosen people from whence the Messiah would come to rescue the nations from the curse of sin and death.

Although this is true, what I find so noteworthy in this story is the fact that the wise men not only understood the significance of Jesus, but that they chose to respond to his significance. The wise men came saying, "Where is he?" They didn't just recognize that he was important; they wanted to be near him. Not only did they desire to be near to him; they desired to worship him.

The whole purpose for the wise men traveling so far was to worship the newborn king.

So the questions rise in our own lives; do we want to be near Jesus? Will Jesus be the affection of our hearts or will he simply be a figure whom we acknowledge during the holiday season? Perhaps we are we too wise, or too busy, to reverence him daily. The wise men did not deem themselves too worthy or knowledgeable to render worship unto the King. We can learn from their example by seeking to understand the importance of Jesus and by responding accordingly to his significance in worship.

....

Father, thank you for sending your Jesus into the world to rescue us. Help us to remember just how important your Son is to our lives and help us to respond to his importance with daily worship. In Jesus' name, Amen.

....

My thoughts and prayers...

THE HOUSE OF BREAD

Jimmy Muir

Matt 2:6 | Micah 5:1-5
'And you, O Bethlehem, in the land of Judah,
*   are by no means least among the rulers of Judah;*
for from you shall come a ruler
*   who will shepherd my people Israel.'*

O little town of Bethlehem
How still we see thee lie
Above thy deep and dreamless sleep
The silent stars go by...

Who doesn't love "O Little Town of Bethlehem"? It is one of the classic Christmas carols. Just like Mary and Joseph, the shepherds and the wise men, the town of Bethlehem plays a significant part in the Christmas story. Why does this little town hold such an important role in the story of Jesus' birth?

The Gospel of Matthew describes the scene when the wise men made their way into Israel. Herod, the ruler in Israel, is freaking out because of the rumors about a new king being born. He summons the local religious leaders to see what they know about where this king might be. They respond by pointing to this prophecy about the Messiah that was written over 700 years before. Bethlehem – a small, insignificant, hillside town – is literally translated "House of Bread."

Yet, hundreds of years earlier, it was prophesied that this rural village would produce the Shepherd which creation long awaited.

This is how God works. He elevates the seemingly weak to demonstrate his strength. He uses the insignificant to point to his glory. Think about the Advent story: a teenage girl, not a queen. A common carpenter, not a king. A dirty stable, not a palace. The House of Bread, not a celestial city.

This was God's plan all along. About thirty years later, the child of that teenage girl and her carpenter husband, the one born in the House of Bread would proclaim these words: "For the bread of God is he who comes down from heaven and gives life to the world." They said to him, "Sir, give us this bread always." Jesus said to them, "I am the bread of life..."

So we celebrate the beauty of God's plan – a plan which he had put into place long before. Bethlehem may not have been much to look at, but God knew something special about this House of Bread – it would bring forth the Bread that would give life to the world.

....

O holy Child of Bethlehem, descend to us, we pray. Cast out our sin and enter in, be born to us today. We hear the Christmas angels the great glad tidings tell. O come to us, abide with us, Our Lord Emmanuel. Amen.

....

My thoughts and prayers...

_____

_____

_____

_____

_____

_____

_____

_____

_____

_____

_____

_____

_____

_____

_____

Fourth Week of
Advent

PEACE WITH GOD

Steve Wright

Luke 2:14
"Glory to God in the highest, and on earth peace among those with whom he is pleased."

I was born during a radical time. The 1960s were a time of rapid change and unrest and in the midst of it a whole generation touted peace. We called them the flower children. They organized peace marches, smoked the peace pipe (or something close to it), and wore the peace sign. They were striving for peace on earth and they're not alone. People today long for peace in the Middle East, peace on our city streets, peace in our homes, and peace in our hearts.

This longing for peace is a symptom of the state of brokenness in which we all live because our sin has separated us from God—who is peace. Fortunately for us, God made a way for us to come back to Him and experience peace on this earth and for all of eternity. When the angels appeared to the shepherds in the field over 2,000 years ago, they announced, "Glory to God in the highest, and on earth peace among those with whom He is pleased" (Luke 2:14). Peace has been available from that day to now, but it is only for those "with whom He is pleased."

So with whom is God pleased? First, God is pleased with His Son, Jesus, whose arrival the shepherds were announcing in the fields that day.

When baby Jesus grows up and obeys God's command to be baptized, God tells Him, "You are my beloved Son; with you I am well pleased" (Luke 3:22). When we repent and believe in the Son, God is then pleased with us because "without faith it is impossible to please him, for whoever would draw near to God must believe that he exists and that he rewards those who seek him" (Hebrews 11:6). There is only one way to seek and know God, and that is through His Son, Jesus. Jesus is the way, the truth, and the life. We can safely conclude that God is pleased with Jesus and all who believe in Him.

Do you want to have peace today? Repent and believe in Jesus. Do you want your family, friends, neighbors and co-workers to have peace today? Then invite them to repent and believe in Jesus.

....

Glory to you, God. Thank you for being pleased to reveal your Son, Jesus, to us. I want to turn from my sin and turn to Jesus today. I believe Jesus died for my sins, was buried, and that God raised Him from the dead so that I could have peace with you. Thank you for that peace and give me your boldness to invite someone to know your peace today. Amen.

....

My thoughts and prayers...

_____

_____

_____

_____

_____

_____

_____

_____

_____

_____

_____

_____

_____

_____

_____

_____

_____

Family Devotion Guide

Based on "Peace With God" by Steve Wright

- Explain that this verse tells us what the angels said when they announced the birth of Jesus.

- Read Luke 2:14:

"Glory to God in the highest, and on earth peace among those with whom he is pleased."

- Discuss: What two things did the angels say?

- Read this passage:

So with whom is God pleased? First, God is pleased with His Son, Jesus, whose arrival the shepherds were announcing in the fields that day. When baby Jesus grows up and obeys God's command to be baptized, God tells Him, "You are my beloved Son; with you I am well pleased" (Luke 3:22). When we repent and believe in the Son, God is then pleased with us because "without faith it is impossible to please him, for whoever would draw near to God must believe that he exists and that he rewards those who seek him" (Hebrews 11:6). There is only one way to seek and know God, and that is through His Son, Jesus. Jesus is the way, the truth, and the life. We can safely conclude that God is pleased with Jesus and all who believe in Him.

- Discuss: What kind of people is God pleased with?

- Read this passage:

Do you want to have peace today? Repent and believe in Jesus. Do you want your family, friends, neighbors and co-workers to have peace today? Then invite them to repent and believe in Jesus.

- Discuss: How can we have peace with God?

- Explain that we can have peace with God when we repent and put our faith in Jesus.

- If any in the family have not placed their faith in Christ, ask them to think about the following prayer as you read it aloud. Then, if they would like to place their faith in Christ, invite them to pray the prayer with you as you read it aloud a second time.*

Dear God, I want to turn from my sin and turn to Jesus today. I believe Jesus died for my sins, was buried, and that God raised Him from the dead so that I could have peace with you. Thank you for that peace. Give me your boldness to invite someone to know your peace today. Amen.

• Play "The First Noel" from Tell the Story Christmas album from Family Church Worship (optional).

To go deeper with family members who are placing their faith in Christ or considering doing so, share the 3 Circles gospel illustration. You can download the 3 Circles app on your phone or tablet (search in the App Store or Google Play store for "Life Conversation Guide").

"I RESEMBLE HEROD"

David Cornett

Matthew 2:7-8
Then Herod summoned the wise men secretly and ascertained
from them what time the star had appeared. And he sent them
to Bethlehem, saying, "Go and search diligently for the child,
and when you have found him, bring me word, that I too may
come and worship him."

Stop and picture Herod for a minute. In my mind, he
embodied every stereotypical image we have of evil. He wore
all the typical villain's attire. I see him with a never-ending
supply of bodyguards…. hundreds of them…with giant, shiny,
bloodthirsty swords. He stood poised to carry out an atrocity
of Biblical proportion. He was the personification of ISIS, but
just two millennia too early. He was the man in charge.

All these details actually happened. Something began that
night that was not of us. A cataclysmic collision between
Herod and the Jews was brewing. The groans of generations
of humanity were heard and heaven's signal flare shown
bright as the tension between the wisdom of this world and
the mercy of God came to a tipping point over a stable in
Bethlehem. Jesus the Messiah was born.

As Herod's deception was spinning, God was still working
out His plan. Truth became flesh and the spirit of wickedness
was illuminated.

Herod's lie, "Go and search so that I may come and worship Him," turned into, "Go and worship so that I might keep searching indefinitely." God was still in control.

As He lived and died and lived again, Jesus showed us that the penalty for our smallest sin is greater than the fruits of humanity's collective self-merit. We, like Herod, have no way out except through Jesus. It's what Herod never lived to understand. And although it's tough to hear it, I know that to a Holy God, without Christ in my life, I resemble Herod. And Jesus still came and cared for me and you so that when we seek Him, we will find Him and worship Him, and praise His name now and forevermore.

....

God, help me to see myself as you truly see me, and be glorified in my life. Thank you for illuminating your truth in my life. Help me to seek you and worship with all my heart. In Jesus' name, Amen.

....

My thoughts and prayers...

_____

_____

_____

_____

_____

_____

_____

_____

_____

_____

_____

_____

_____

_____

_____

_____

STEPPING BACK

Keith Albert

Matthew 2:9-10
After listening to the king, they went on their way. And behold, the star that they had seen when it rose went before them until it came to rest over the place where the child was. When they saw the star, they rejoiced exceedingly with great joy.

Did the star stop moving because the wise men had arrived in Jerusalem? Could they have found their way by just following the star without the King's direction? We do not know. Yet, when they arrived in Jerusalem, they realized no one else was looking for the King of the Jews. A complacent religious community searched the scriptures to tell a scheming King that Bethlehem was the Child's birthplace. The King gave instructions to the wise men and off they went.

As they headed toward Bethlehem, the star reappeared and their rejoicing exploded into "great joy"! They were "busting at the seams"! Their joy could not be contained; it was 'over the top'. Interestingly, their joy was expressed by faith, since they had not yet seen Jesus.

Seeking Christ through scripture leads us into His presence. Yet, we can be easily distracted from what God wants to reveal to us.

Several years ago my sister-in-law celebrated her wedding with a late night reception around a bonfire at the beach.

We had a blast among the joyful conversations taking place around the fire. Midway through the celebration, I walked away from the circle of family toward the water, away from the warmth and glow of the fire. I was stunned. Being so close to the comfort of the fire, friends, and family, prevented me from seeing the splendor and wonder of God's creation displayed against a dark, cloudless night. I had to step away from the familiar in order to see the glory of God.

This Christmas, immerse yourself in the reading of scripture (Matthew, Mark, Luke or John). Leave the familiar, leave complacency, leave scheming and simply enjoy the season with "great joy" in the presence of Christ.

....

Father, I am so easily distracted. Renew my steps toward you. Bring this "great joy" into my life as I seek your presence through the guidance and reading of scripture. As the star led the wise men, help me to step back and look up so that I can focus on you. Help me to see and be obedient to where you are leading me. Amen.

....

My thoughts and prayers...

JESUS THE CENTER

Christian Ramos

Matthew 2:11
And going into the house they saw the child with Mary his mother, and they fell down and worshiped him. Then, opening their treasures, they offered him gifts, gold and frankincense and myrrh.

Growing up, I always looked forward to Christmastime. There was just something special about the family getting together, singing songs, giving and receiving gifts, and, of course, eating food. The little things my parents did for us every year became traditions, and today my wife and I do them for our children.

Many of our Christmas traditions resemble those of most families. We go to a relative's house to be together with other family members and once we are there, we open gifts and offer gifts to others. When we read this passage, we see the wise men doing the very same thing. The scripture says that they went into the house, saw the child, and opened and offered their gifts. Right in the middle of all of this, they fell down and worshiped Jesus.

Christmas traditions are a blessing. It's good to look forward to them, but let's not forget to give Jesus His rightful place in the center of it all. The wise men could have just visited Jesus and not worshiped Him, yet they chose to make the worship of God Incarnate the focus of their visit. Their encounter with Jesus changed everything. Their search was not in vain.

They found the One who would deliver them from their brokenness. Their gifts were no longer just an empty gesture. They were given as an expression of belief in Jesus as the Son of God, given to Him who is the greatest gift to all of humanity. They were offered to Him who would give the gift of life and salvation to a dying world.

Christmas is an opportunity for each of us to put Jesus in the center of our hearts. Let's make the worship of Jesus the center of all our traditions. Let's make the worship of Jesus the center of our lives this year.

....

Lord, as we experience the beauty of this season, please motivate us to purposely place you in the center of all our traditions. As we seek to give and receive, grant us the willingness to give and receive more of you. Help us to place you in the center of our lives and to allow your presence to give meaning to every aspect of this season and the days that follow. Amen.

....

My thoughts and prayers...

THE FLIGHT TO EGYPT

Jimmy Fogleman

Matthew 2:13-15
Now when they had departed, behold, an angel of the Lord
appeared to Joseph in a dream and said, "Rise, take the child
and his mother, and flee to Egypt, and remain there until I
tell you, for Herod is about to search for the child, to destroy
him." And he rose and took the child and his mother by night
and departed to Egypt and remained there until the death
of Herod. This was to fulfill what the Lord had spoken by the
prophet, "Out of Egypt I called my son."

One of the most exciting times in the lives of any couple is the
arrival of their first baby. The new parents now have a blessed
addition to take care of and to nurture. This is a time to
celebrate and rejoice; to document and share every noise,
movement, or anything new that happens with family and
friends. These moments are to be cherished and remembered
as they pass so quickly.

But it wasn't like this for Mary and Joseph, the new parents of
their firstborn, Jesus.

Having a child was different for them, right from the
beginning when the announcement of Mary's pregnancy
came through an angel. Now, in this passage, another angel
comes to warn the couple of the impending danger. Now they
are on the run to save the child's life.

Herod was ruthless in his quest to remain in power; when he heard the "King of the Jews" had been born he would not sit idly by. He sought to destroy the child. Yet, in the midst of it all, God had a plan to fulfill, which He had set forth before the beginning of time.

Sometimes we get so overwhelmed with the circumstances of the moment we can forget that God is not overwhelmed by anything. He was going to take care of His only Son so He could grow up to do what God had sent Him to do – "take away the sin of the world." (John 1:29) You can see even in these few verses how God was orchestrating, guiding, and providing a way for Mary and Joseph to take care of their firstborn. God is no different today as He will do the same for those who "love Him and are called according His purpose." (Romans 8:28) We are to walk closely with God, love Him with all of our heart, and follow Him no matter what.

....

Dear Father, I know you love me and I know you have promised to take care of me every step of the way. Please give me the courage to trust you when things seem so hard, to obey you when things don't make sense, and to follow you wherever you lead me. Amen.

....

My thoughts and prayers...

Christmas Eve / Christmas Day

GOD CAME DOWN

Bernie Cueto

John 1:1-5, 14
In the beginning was the Word, and the Word was with God,
and the Word was God. He was in the beginning with God.
All things were made through him and without him was not
anything made that was made. In him was life, and the life
was the light of men. The light shines in the darkness, and the
darkness has not overcome it.

And the Word became flesh and dwelt among us, and we have
seen his glory, glory as of the only Son from the Father, full of
grace and truth.

Christmas is a season when we spend time with friends and
family who mean the most to us. We often focus on lights to
hang, trees to decorate, and gifts to purchase and distribute.
Yet, Christmas is about much more than lights, trees, and gifts.

The beginning of John's Gospel is one of the most beautiful
passages in all of Scripture. It offers us a helpful reminder
of who we should focus on this Christmas. It focuses on God
himself in the person of Jesus Christ, the Light of the World.
Jesus never wrote a song, yet more songs are written about
Him than any other person in history. He never authored a
book, but books about Him can fill warehouses. The
incarnation, his arrival on earth, served to divide the whole
of human history in two (B.C. and A.D.).

He calmed seas, healed the hurting, challenged the comfortable, comforted the challenged, and changed every life he touched. It is no surprise that even His own disciples said, "Who is this Jesus?"

John 1:1-5 declares that Jesus Christ did not make His debut on that first Christmas morning in Bethlehem. He existed before creation—"in the beginning," and "through Him all things were made" (John 1:1, 3). In Genesis God said, "Let us make man in our image" (Genesis 1:26). God the Father speaking to God the Son, the Word! The Word is none other than Jesus Christ. We know this because later, in verse 14, John tells us, "The Word became flesh and dwelt among us." Can you imagine? The Eternal Word, God, came down to dwell among us! One translation states, "The Word became human and made his home among us." God wanted to reveal Himself to us in terms we could understand. One preacher said, "Jesus took everything there was to know about God and put it on a shelf we could reach."

....

Heavenly Father, may I focus on Christ this Christmas, the One who has lit my heart by grace through faith. Help me to not focus so much on the decorative lights that I forget about the Light of the World. Help me not obsess so much about the tree that I forget that He suffered on a tree for my sins. May I not become so burdened with gifts that I forget about the greatest gift of all, the gift of salvation. Thank you that I can celebrate Him who made His home among us so that I can know you. Amen.

....

My thoughts and prayers...

_____

_____

_____

_____

_____

_____

_____

_____

_____

_____

_____

_____

_____

_____

Family Devotion Guide

Based on "God Came Down" by Bernie Cueto

(Suggested to use on Christmas Eve or Christmas Day)

Optional materials: a candle and a way to light it.

- Read John 1:1-5, 14:

In the beginning was the Word, and the Word was with God, and the Word was God. He was in the beginning with God. All things were made through him and without him was not anything made that was made. In him was life, and the life was the light of men. The light shines in the darkness, and the darkness has not overcome it.

And the Word became flesh and dwelt among us, and we have seen his glory, glory as of the only Son from the Father, full of grace and truth.

- Read the following passage:

Christmas is a season when we spend time with friends and family who mean the most to us. We often focus on lights to hang, trees to decorate, and gifts to purchase and distribute. Yet, Christmas is about much more than lights, trees, and gifts.

The beginning of John's Gospel is one of the most beautiful passages in all of Scripture. It offers us a helpful reminder of who we should focus on this Christmas.

It focuses on God himself in the person of Jesus Christ, the Light of the World. Jesus never wrote a song, yet more songs are written about Him than any other person in history. He never authored a book, but books about Him can fill warehouses. The incarnation, his arrival on earth, served to divide the whole of human history in two (B.C. and A.D.). He calmed seas, healed the hurting, challenged the comfortable, comforted the challenged, and changed every life he touched. It is no surprise that even His own disciples said, "Who is this Jesus?"

John 1:1-5 declares that Jesus Christ did not make His debut on that first Christmas morning in Bethlehem. He existed before creation—"in the beginning," and "through Him all things were made" (John 1:1, 3). In Genesis God said, "Let us make man in our image" (Genesis 1:26). God the Father speaking to God the Son, the Word! The Word is none other than Jesus Christ. We know this because later, in verse 14, John tells us, "The Word became flesh and dwelt among us." Can you imagine? The Eternal Word, God, came down to dwell among us! One translation states, "The Word became human and made his home among us." God wanted to reveal Himself to us in terms we could understand. One preacher said, "Jesus took everything there was to know about God and put it on a shelf we could reach."

- Discuss: Why do we celebrate Christmas?

- Light a candle, explaining that it represents Jesus as the Light of the World.

- Play "Silent Night" from Tell the Story Christmas album from Family Church Worship (optional).

- Have a family member read this prayer aloud:

Heavenly Father, may we focus on Christ this Christmas, the One who has lit our hearts by grace through faith. Help us to not focus so much on the decorative lights that we forget about the Light of the World. Help us not obsess so much about the tree that we forget that He suffered on a tree for our sins. May we not become so burdened with gifts that we forget about the greatest gift of all, the gift of salvation. Thank you that we can celebrate Him who made His home among us so that we can know you. Amen.

HATED FROM BIRTH

Steven Madonna

Matthew 2:16-18
Then Herod, when he saw that he had been tricked by the wise men, became furious and he sent and killed all the male children in Bethlehem and in all that region who were two years old and under, according to the time that he had ascertained from the wise men. Then was fulfilled what was spoken by the prophet Jeremiah: "A voice was heard in Ramah, weeping and loud lamentation, Rachel weeping for her children; she refused to be comforted, because they are no more."

When most of us think of Christmas, we picture stockings, chestnuts roasting, and visions of sugar plums dancing in our heads—all associated with the wonderful cozy image of the infant Jesus, nestling safely in swaddling clothes and lying in a manger. We don't picture the murderous threats of King Herod towards the newly born Savior of the world, and the slaughter of innocent Hebrew infants. However, a Christmas narrative without this part of the story robs us of important insights about our Lord and His mission.

First, our Lord was opposed from birth. He was in danger and fighting from the moment of his arrival. Jesus' birth was the spiritual equivalent of Allied forces setting foot on the sands of Normandy. He was met with immediate hatred and opposition by the evil powers of this world. The prophet Moses was opposed at birth in the same way by the Egyptian Pharaoh.

Second, Jesus isn't just similar to Moses, but greater than Moses, One who all of Scripture points to. Remember the words of Genesis 3, that the child of the woman will crush the head of the serpent? There is a satanic spirit at work in the sons of disobedience which, like Herod, seeks the destruction of infants and innocent human life since it was an infant that brought their demise.

This Christmas season, let us remember that Jesus, our God and Savior, came on a mission to destroy the works of the devil (1 John 3:8), and that he was violently opposed by this world. Therefore we, within whom the Spirit of Christ dwells, should not expect anything different. However let us not lose heart but continue to hope in King Jesus and His gospel.

....

Heavenly Father, I pray that you would continuously cover us with your grace and mercy. Give us strength through your Holy Spirit that indwells us. Please enable us to have courage in the face of a word that boldly opposes your church, your Gospel, and your Son most of all—our Lord and Savior Jesus Christ. Amen.

....

My thoughts and prayers...

_____

_____

_____

_____

_____

_____

_____

_____

_____

_____

_____

_____

_____

_____

_____

_____

LISTEN AND OBEY

Charbel Khadij

Matthew 2:19-20
After Herod died, an angel of the Lord appeared in a dream
to Joseph in Egypt and said, "Get up, take the child and his
mother and go to the land of Israel, for those who were trying
to take the child's life are dead."

After King Herod died, the angel of the Lord came to Joseph in a dream. God spoke to him in a unique way. What can we learn from the example of Joseph? Joseph was a God fearing man. He was a man whose heart was willing to serve the Lord. Through faith he knew God was working through the situation, and that God's plan, the birth of Jesus Christ, was coming to pass. Joseph, in obedience, responded to God when he was called to go and to leave his home, friends, and family. I love how Joseph responded immediately. When God said go, he went. He was pursuing a mission God entrusted him with.

It's easy to wonder if we are still a part of God's plan. We hear from God once and obey, but then what? Are we exactly where God wants us to be? His Word says, "Be still and know that I am God." You can trust that if things change, God can speak again in a unique, clear way just like the first time He spoke. God has no difficulty speaking in a way we will understand. We need to be willing to listen—and obey—just like Joseph. When God calls us, we should respond.

Notice that God communicated to Joseph through multiple dreams. God works uniquely with each individual; He speaks to each of us in a special way. How amazing it is that we serve a God who has a perfect plan and works behind the scenes. Many times we cannot see what He is doing. Know that God has a plan for you. Ask yourself: do you trust the plan He has for you? Are you willing to go when He calls? Are you willing to be obedient and pursue the mission God gives you? Let go and let God—He will take care of everything along the way.

....

Lord, make me a faithful servant of your truth and your word. Help me to obey you willingly, just like Joseph, with complete trust and with a joyful heart. Help me remember that you are in control, and that your plan is perfect. Thank you for your love for me. I pray I would be obedient and respond when you call. Amen.

....

My thoughts and prayers...

_____

_____

_____

_____

_____

_____

_____

_____

_____

_____

_____

_____

_____

_____

_____

_____

_____

NO MORE TEARS

Kevin Mahoney

Revelation 21:4
He will wipe every tear from their eyes. There will be no more
death or mourning or crying or pain, for the old order of things
has passed away.

"Joy to the World, the Lord is come! Let earth receive her King;
let every heart prepare Him room, and Heaven and nature
sing!" Thoughts of Christmas resound with these words.

Yet, despite the fact that joy and happiness are so often
associated with Christmas, the reality is that for many,
Christmas is the most difficult time of year. Many people
experience more sadness, depression, and loneliness during
this festive time of year than any other season. The holidays
are painful reminders of loved ones we have lost. We miss
them and wonder how we can be happy without them. When
our family relationships are out of sorts, we feel it more
acutely at Christmastime. And some people simply have no
one to celebrate with.

While many eyes sparkle with the lights and scenes of
Christmas, many eyes are full of tears of sorrow. Such a
contrast – sparkling eyes and crying eyes.

For those who believe in the baby born in a manger—who would become the Lamb of God who was crucified, died and was buried, and three days later rose from the dead—there is a day coming when there will be no more crying. No more crying eyes—only eyes that sparkle as they gaze at a Glorified King. That is the real joy of Christmas.

No more tears – Joy to the World!!!

....

Lord Jesus, I long for the day when you will make everything new. Fill me with the joy of my salvation and constantly remind me that "those who sow in tears will reap with songs of joy" (Isaiah 12:5). Amen.

....

My thoughts and prayers...

APPENDIX ONE

How to have a devotional time with God.

Some Christians are very familiar with the practice of a daily devotional time, but if you are new to following Jesus or just out of the habit, you might find these guidelines helpful.

- First, find a place that is comfortable and free from distractions, where you can focus on God. Silence your phone, turn off the TV.

- Ideally, choose a time when you are mentally alert. Many people prefer to have their devotionals in the morning to start their day off right, but if you are not a morning person, later in the day might work better.

- Do not worry too much about how much time you spend. Start with just 5 or 10 minutes and let it grow naturally.

- Being consistent every day is more important than how much time you spend. If you are just establishing the daily devotional habit, you are better off spending 5 minutes every day for 7 days than spending 30 minutes on Wednesday and Friday.

- It's common during devotional time to find your mind wandering to things you have to do. If that happens, try keeping a sheet of paper close by. When you remember something, jot it down, then bring your focus back to God.

A successful devotional consists of reading and thinking about God's word, and taking time to pray.

To get you started, here is a suggested outline for a 10 minute devotional time.

1 minute: Make sure you have what you need: your Bible, devotional book, and a pen. Take one minute to settle your mind and focus. Take a few deep breaths and remember that God is with you.

5 minutes: Read through the Scripture passage and reflection for the day. This will take you less than five minutes, so after your first read-through, go back to the scripture and read through again, slowly. I suggest you read with a pen or pencil, and underline anything that seems to stand out to you. Trust the Holy Spirit to guide you as you read and to speak to you through the text. Feel free to write notes or prayers in the devotional book—it's yours and there is no rule against it!

4 minutes: Pray. You may begin with the suggested prayer, but don't stop there—keep praying. You might pray about what you sensed from the Lord during your reading. Pray about the day ahead of you: things you have to do and the people you will see. Pray for your family and neighbors.

Remember, prayer is simply talking with God. There are no rules. Say to Him what is on your heart, and take time to listen also. Be open to having the Holy Spirit guide you as to what to pray about.

At the end of your prayer time, express thanks to the Lord, then get on with your day.

Remember: the goal of the devotional time is relationship. You are there to love God and to hear from Him, not to force yourself to do a religious duty. If you are new to it, it may feel awkward at first. Try not to worry about whether you are "doing it right." Focus on loving God and listening to Him. After a few times, you will find it becoming more and more natural.

APPENDIX TWO

How to Lead a Family Devotional Time

Many parents feel unqualified to lead a time of family devotions or family worship. Sometimes we think we have to be Bible experts or child psychologists even to attempt it. The truth is, it's not complicated at all. If you read part of the Bible, talk about what it means and pray together, you've done what it takes.

We've set up our five Family Devotional Guides to be short and as simple as possible, and to not require much preparation.

Children will remember what they learn during a family devotional time, but the most powerful lesson will be the example of their parents leading them towards God.

Consider the suggestions below:

1. Do the family devotional at dinner time. Dinner is a good excuse for the entire family to be together in the same place at the same time. Given how most families' schedules tend to be, trying to set up a separate devotional time may be difficult.

2. Consider starting with some informal conversation about what's going on in each person's life as dinner begins. When everyone is over halfway done with their meal, transition to the devotional time.

3. Aim for once a week. You can certainly have family devotions more often, but that may not work for everyone. We've set up this book to have a family devotion on Sunday for four weeks, but any day can work. For the Advent season, try picking a day and meal time that can be consistent for the four weeks. The last Family Devotion Guide is designed to be used either on Christmas Eve or Christmas Day, whichever works best for your family.

4. The Family Devotion Guides in this book are just that—guides. You do not have to do everything suggested. Your kids may be too old or young for some of what we suggest. Feel free to change up the discussion questions as well as add or subtract certain activities.

5. Do not feel like a Family Devotional needs to take a long time. Shorter is better. Rather than having kids sitting impatiently through an over-long devotional, keeping the lesson shorter helps retain attention and may even provide "space" for extra thoughts and questions.

6. Use the devotional time to give older children an opportunity to read, to lead discussion, to pray, or to help (like playing the songs). Giving them these leadership opportunities helps them begin to lead and serve.

7. Finally, keep it fun! Family devotions don't need to be overly serious. If children enjoy the devotional times, they will look forward to doing them again. Encourage a positive atmosphere.

Don't miss our companion Christmas album

"Tell the Story"

8 songs in English | 6 songs in Spanish

available at